BEING TOGETHER BUT FEELING ALONE FROM NARCISSISTIC ABUSE

PATRICIA CLARK

Patricia Clark
Being together but feeling alone from Narcissistic Abuse

All rights reserved
Copyright © 2024 by **Patricia Clark**

Published by Spines
ISBN: 979-8-89383-607-3

CONTENTS

INTRODUCTION

I have asked myself so many times, how did I get to this place in my life where I feel like I do not know myself anymore? It is like you are living in morning fog dealing with a narcissist. I was in a relationship for over a decade before I found out that it was the name of all the turmoil I was going through. I think because of my past childhood trauma, I had learned to accept toxicity for normalcy. When I would speak to my mother about the way I felt as a child she would flip the subject on her then start telling me how she went through trauma as a child. So, you mean to tell me that your past trauma caused you to mistreat your children and not give them the love, affection, and attention that they deserve? I get it. Childhood trauma is very painful, but we all have been through several types of trauma in our lives. You would think if a person knew the way it feels you should not want anyone else to feel that type of pain. My mother kept us in competition with each other while going back and forth with the he says she says trying to tear us apart for her to gain control over our minds. Ladies, I just want to say, even though this book is talking about dealing with a male narcissist, I want to add that there is such a thing as a female narcissist as well out here in this world with the same characteristics as the male. I am just giving my experience of dealing with a male narcissist. I understand now that my mother is a narcissist along with ex- narc, ex- friends, and family members after watching so many videos and doing my research on narcissist abuse. I have come to realize why I stayed in that dysfunctional relationship for so long enduring the cruel punishment and heart ache. I had been dealing with gaslighting, lack of empathy, frequent envy, never admitting fault, bullying, co-dependency, neediness, passive aggressiveness, and manipulative behaviors all my life. I also read that children of narcissists' parents often end up in codependent relationships with people who have narcissistic traits or become a narcissist themselves. It still blows my mind till this day, how you can have two children that grow up in the same household enduring similar trauma but one becomes an empath while the other child becomes a narcissist. The children feel like they can never be good enough for their partner or themselves, so they become codependent on other people to make them happy and validate their self-worth. As much as it hurts to think that I was once in this state of mind, I do agree with the information I read and watched.

1

NARCISSISTIC PEOPLE COME OFF AS CHARMING INDIVIDUALS

My friends used to always tell me that my mother was such a nice lady. I remember thinking yell right, only if you know the real person behind that smile and her being soft spoken. Narcissistic people come off as nice individuals is until you get to know them. They are very charming and attractive and take immense pride in their appearance. This is one of the tools they use to bait you into their world of confusion and pain.

2

LOVE BOOMING PHASE

I met this man while starting a new job. I remember sitting on a bench my first day of work waiting for my trainer when this work van showed up and this fellow jumped out and came over to me and introduced himself and stated that he was going to be my trainer for that night. I had so much going on in my life at that time and he came across as someone I could talk to. He was very attentive and seemed to be an empathic individual. By the time we got off he asked me if I had a ride home. I told him no. So, he offered me a ride home. We exchanged numbers for that purpose and for a brief period he became my ride back and forth to work. Then we started stopping for breakfast after work. Eventually we started hanging out with each other outside of work. Everything played out so fast. I regret not turning away from him when he wanted to have a sexual intercourse with me, and I told him that I already had children and I was not looking for a one-night stand. His response was that he was not ready for a commitment at that time so I told him we could not see each other again because we were looking for two separate things. If I knew my worth back, then I would have walked away and never looked back. But I did not ... days went by and then he called me to tell me he was ready for the commitment that I wanted. We started hanging out again with each other, taking beautiful pictures throughout town. We were inseparable. The funny thing that I noticed about him is that when I would break it off with him because he did something that I was not okay with, the same pictures we had taken years ago enjoying each other were the pictures he would send to my phone. Now I know it is because they try to remind you about how life used to be with them so you can think about the great times that you shared and long for those memories to return. Ladies, you will never get that person back that you saw in the beginning because that was not their true self. They were grooming you to later make you wish for more of the potential person you saw in the beginning every time you want to walk away from them because they have treated you badly. They knew that day would come just like the other people that had walked out of their lives. Also, during the love bomb phase, they make you feel sexy, attractive, beautiful, and safe. I even assumed because of the excessive texting that he was really feeling me. I had no idea this was a tactic of theirs to hook their victims for them to let their guards down so they could gain control over them. You think because he can send you so many text messages throughout the day as if you are the only one on his mind no baby that is not the case. They are great liars and cheaters. They will text other women while sitting in the same room as you. So that does not mean anything to a narcissist. If they think they have met their true soulmate they will even text and call the new supply while you are sleeping. I just want to add because I share children with my ex-narc he would come over to my home to spend time with our children while trying to love bomb me saying how he wants his family back while texting his new girlfriend. I know this is a fact because I saw her calling his phone but he wouldn't pick it up because he was over to my house but shortly after that I saw him texting her back when the love bombing did not work for me. Never get mad because they have wronged you or left you and you think they are going to treat the next woman better. Trust me, what you are seeing is what they showed you at the beginning. Give it some time their relationship with the other woman is going to run its course you know why, because you are a great woman you were never the problem it was because of his pain and insecurities that he inflicted on you that made you set boundaries which caused him to move on to the next person. Soon you are later, he is going to treat her the same exact way he treated you.

3
DO NOT IGNORE THE RED FLAG

Ladies, the red flags are there to let you know that something is not right. Ignoring them will cause you pain later in the relationship. Like the things they do that will have you puzzled or confused. Are if you see something that they did wrong but act like it is no big deal or start gaslighting yourself saying it is no big deal you will let it slide but they better not do it again are you will leave. I want you to know that thinking like that will have you stuck for so many years in an unhealthy situation. These types of people love playing mind games with you and if you let them get away once they will continue to mistreat you. They think that because you gave them another chance you are OK with their bad behaviors, and you will not leave them. The only way they will respect you is if you set clear boundaries and stick to them. I want you to save years of your life, do not waste them like I did being in a relationship that will eventually end because the narcissist had bad intentions from the start.

4
GIVING THEM CHILDREN

Having a child with a narcissist is one of the biggest mistakes you could ever make. They give us a child to gain a lifetime supply if we allow it. He would always make comments like I do not care who you get with I hold the prize I gave you two children they could never give you that. I love my babies dearly. They are my world. But I promise this man has tried to make my life a living hell through my children. Due to their lack of empathy, they manipulate their children. He used to buy our daughter her favorite toys or foods to get information from her or for him to be able to go through my phone while she was using it. I would tell him I wanted to feed the kids healthier. He would buy them unhealthy snacks just to make me look like a bad parent so he could gain favor from them. A narc will try to exploit your children for their benefit. I used to try to leave him. He would say things like you cannot take my children away from me. I am going to put out a warrant on you for kidnapping my children. He would threaten me by saying he is going to take me to court and fight to get custody of them because I am unfit, unstable, and need mental help. All these unkind words they will project onto you to make you question your sanity or cause you to have low self-esteem. They know you are nothing like them and you genuinely love your children and will do anything in your power to take care of them and keep them safe. That is why they try to use those tactics thinking that you will stay in a toxic environment out of fear of losing your children to them. I got so tired of him threatening me about what he would do if I left him, I decided to play his game. I said because I know you are using the children to keep me here acting like you want your children around, but you are never home and do not spend any time nor do anything with them. I can't stay in this relationship any longer. I'll leave them with you for a few months to go and get myself together because I have to start over from scratch and then come back for them. His whole attitude changed. I never had a problem with him threatening to take them from me again. I left him three times and each time I was able to take the children because he did not want that responsibility. The household will never be a family unit if the Narcissist is up under the same roof. You will try to discipline your children by teaching them the difference between right and wrong, then here comes the narcissist with their negative input. They are always negative and working against you and trying to turn the kids against you. I will advise all the women that have children that are old enough to remember the narcissist behaviors to get them into counseling so they can become productive adults and not have to live the same life as their fathers.

5

THEIR LACK OF EMPATHY CAUSES PAIN FOR THEIR CHILD

The children love their father which they should the same way the child loves their mother. My daughter would jump into his arms when he walked into the house. She was so excited to see him. Only for him to barely hug her before rushing about with his day because he had already made plans. My baby would beg him to take her to the park, to the movies, or for him to just spend the day with her. Sometimes after he had upset her, he would call his self-spending time with her continuously being on his phone staring off into space with deep thoughts. He would make promises to her that he would not keep. After a while, our oldest child stopped believing in him and did not care about spending time with him anymore. But our youngest continued to want to be around him because she was getting material things from him instead of genuine quality time and at her age, she associated that with love. I had to teach her the difference between the two.

6

THE COURT SYSTEM FAILS OUR CHILDREN AND NON-NARCISSISTIC PARENTS

My take on the court system is that the people that they have in place to oversee divorce cases sometimes do not favor the best interest of the children. Women may not have been married to their child's father but simply had to file for child support, sole custody, or supervised visitation due to the father's lack of trying to co-parent. I just can't understand if I'm explaining to you how this man has abused me the entire relationship while my children had to watch and hear the cruel behaviors of the narcissist, but you expect me to want to share custody with someone that I know could do more damage to my children. What kind of system do we have? If you are not protecting our babies, you are putting them in harm's way and failing them. I am not saying fathers should never be able to spend time with or see their children, but some fathers do not even know what is best for themselves so how are they going to raise their children? If we do not advocate for our children not only will the system fail them, but then we will also lose them. We must protect our children and not be afraid to speak out about this abuse so we can bring more awareness to the community and court systems so we can protect children.

7
THE FIRST TIME I FOUND OUT ABOUT HIM CHEATING

After moving in with me he took a job offering decent wages, so that gave him more money to wine and dine with the ladies. At that time, I noticed that he started staying out late at night sometimes not even coming home. He would come home with hickeys on his neck and when I would question him about them, he would say that he works with fiber glass and when it hits his neck it causes red spots because his skin was so light. Ladies, sometimes we gaslight ourselves because we love our mate and do not want to believe the truth that lies right in front of us. There I was around seven months pregnant with a man that showed no interest in me. We purchased a car together but on Valentine's Day the car was impounded because he allowed my cousin to use it and my cousin called me from jail telling me to tell my boyfriend that the car was impounded. My boyfriend never knew because he was out with his new supplies. So, when he came home, I told him about the car. He never got the car out, but I did because I had other children that I needed to care for, and I used the car to get back and forth to my doctors' appointments. I will never forget the day I picked the car up from the impound, pulled the sun visor down and two Valentine cards fell into my lap. I opened the cards and they read ... I am glad that I met you. I enjoy spending time with you, and I look forward to spending more time with you. Then he signed his name. I knew they were not for me because he had given me a card on Valentine's Day along with something to eat before he left the house, and he signed it by saying love then his name. Two weeks later I had an appointment to find out what the sex of our child was. He never showed up. Later, I found a receipt from him shopping at the mall with the same date and time that I had my ultrasound. One month later he came home with a name he wanted me to name our son. I even thought about naming our son that name until I received a call from this other woman telling me that her and my child's father had a fling and that she was the one that had given him the name for our son. I knew that she was telling the truth because she said the same name that he asked me to give our son. She even said that she was in love with her child's father and that my child's father was a good man. I remember thinking... He is a good man, but I am eight months pregnant, and he is out sleeping with another woman, but he is a great man. Chuckle .... One day while we were riding in the car, we stopped by CVS to pick up my medicine. I recall him going inside to get it. When he returned to the car, he looked over at me and said that he was in love with two women. He then said it was me and another woman. I was so devastated. At that time, I told him about the conversation I had with the other woman and how she said he was just a fling and that she was in love with her child's father. For a second, I watched him crumble into pieces like how he had just left my heart.

8

FLYING MONKEYS

When a narcissist starts to discard you, they start a smear campaign. They start telling people that the reason they are leaving the relationship is because you have mental issues, cheating on them, being lazy, does not treat them well, does not keep the house clean, doesn't take care of the kids, or you don't want anything out of life. All along, they are the ones taking you through hell by degrading you, cheating on you, lying, abandoning you and the children. When I was pregnant with our first child, he found a new supply and started smearing my name to his mother and sister stating that I was cheating on him so when I had our child his mother came to the hospital and examined our child from head to toe. He later told me that she said that our child did not look like him. Now that I know that he is a liar I doubt what he said or she said. Even if she said that I am not upset with her because he planted that seed in her mind way before our child was born. So, she walked into that hospital room with uncertainty already on her mind. I remember one time the narc told me that a supply that he was messing with told him that his wife did a number on him. I guess because she saw that he was angry, mentally unstable, mean, and started to treat her badly she assumed that his behaviors came from me mistreating him. She had no idea that his mask had spilled and that was his true color. Also, that let me know that he had conversations about me with her and told her lies about me if she thought his behavior was from what I took him through. Boy oh boy was she in for a rude awakening. Also, one day he told me that he is a secretive person and that he does not like putting his business on the street. So, I respected his wishes and kept the things he did to me private and would not speak to anyone about the way he treated me. Ladies, this is a big mistake let me tell you why, because the narcissist is out here dragging your name through the mud to everyone that you know making you look like the monster all the while we are sitting back protecting their image from the world while suffering in silence. So, when we do speak out about the problem no one believes us unless they have experienced this type of abuse themselves.

9

HOOVERING ONCE YOU DECIDE TO LEAVE

After you make up your mind to leave them, they will give you excessive attention until they get you back. Every time you go back, they will mistreat you and discard you again. It is a game for them. I remember one day he told me when we broke up that making up was the best part. I cannot speak for everyone else but once I went back, I tried to be the best version of myself each time because I felt like I was in competition with the other women. I left because I found out that he was having an affair. So, I tried to give him great sex, keep the house clean, cook more for him, take care of the kids by myself, support him while putting my life on the back burner. It seems like they really do not want to much out of life but to run the streets having affairs on their wives or significant other, drugs, gambling, and the list goes on. Once you leave them that is when they start saying things like I will go to counseling. I never meant to hurt you. I only wanted to give you the world. By that time, we start feeling sorry for them. Then we start thinking about the things we could change about ourselves that would make the relationship better. I completely lost myself in that relationship. The truth is they were the problem, we were never the problem. So, if we continue to fault ourselves for their behaviors thinking that we are the reason they behave the way that they do they will never change. They will continue to walk around getting away with their harmful behaviors if we keep blaming ourselves for the way they treat us. We must start making them take accountability for their actions and stop allowing them to show us who they are more than once. I am not saying we are perfect no one is perfect that is walking this earth is. We all make mistakes but there is a difference between a mistake and a pattern. A mistake is once you do it you correct the problem, a pattern is something you do repeatedly without any remorse.

10

NO GROWTH DURING THE ENTIRE RELATIONSHIP

Never give your power to someone who is not sure of their own decision making. Actions speak louder than words. I have always been a go-getter, but I could not understand why I could not seem to get on my feet with him. It seems like once I take one step forward, I will take ten steps back. I did not realize he was working against me instead of with me. I used to sit down with him and make plans on how we were going to work together to become financially stable. Everything would be good for about a week then everything would fall apart. I supported this man in every way that I knew how. Putting my dreams and goals on the back burner because I felt once I helped him with his career, I could execute mine. Every time I would tell him about a career move I wanted to make, he would always be so negative about it I would lose interest doubting myself thinking that this is not the right time because I was looking for that support and validation from him. I trusted his judgement and advice on so many things even though at times it did not sit well with me. They do not want you to have more or do better than them. They want to keep you dependent on them so they can maintain control over you.

11

THE NARCISSISTS VIEW YOU AS AN OPPORTUNITY AND PLOT TO USE YOU TO GET AHEAD IN LIFE

When a narcissist meets you and starts talking to you, they already start to size you up to see if they can take advantage of you. That is why they ask so many questions at the beginning because they are trying to find out as much as possible about your present, past, and future. They gather all your information only to use it against you eventually. Say for instance you told them how you came into a lawsuit for whatever reason, and you told them you used some of the money to help your ex start a construction business, but the business went under because the ex got hooked on drugs and no longer has the business. They will say things like he was a fool and I would never mess up that opportunity all the while trying to figure out if you had more money, they could get it firsthand. Say you come from a family where you were the black sheep of the family, but they see it does not matter what you have been through. You are still strong, determined, and successful despite your past. They would come off like they are caring and say, I hate that you had to endure that kind of treatment as a child. You did not deserve that. They will even make you think that you are safe with them now and they will never leave you like other people have done to you in your past. So, they can break down your walls that you have put up for protection. While they are sitting back waiting for the chance to hurt and take advantage of you as well. There were so many times I would hear the narcissist I had in my life contemplate how he was going to make money off me once we divorced. He said things like Mary J Blige's husband taking shots at her situation with her ex-husband which made me furious. How do you feel you are entitled to anything when the only thing you did in this relationship was cause pain and take? Narcissistic people do not help you build. They are only there to take everything that they can. I found myself waiting to start my business that I have always wanted to start until our divorce would be final because I knew the only thing that he was relying on was taking everything that he could from me that he did not deserve. I was a hair braider for years with excellent clientele. I used to tell him that I wanted to own a braiding shop. He would say there is no money in braiding hair. You should take a job that has great benefits. I would say to him that I could buy health and life insurance. He still would have a problem with it but never had a problem with going with me to spend the money I made from braiding hair. After he realized that I was leaving him he finally came to me telling me how smart I was, and we could make money together so much as starting a business. Guess what business he wanted to start with me? You guessed it opening a salon. Something that I tried to do the entire time I was with him.

12

SEX WITH A NARCISSIST

Narcissists use sex to gain control. Have you noticed that when you are intimate with a narcissist it seems like their mind is in another place? I even noticed that right after a bad argument they will try to have sex with you and during sex they will try to control you saying things like this is my **** and you better not give it to anybody else. All the while they are the ones that are running around all over town sleeping with women that will allow them to sleep with them. They try to make you apologize for what they have done to you. They will even do the unthinkable things and request you to perform degrading acts on them during sex. Majority of them are addicted to pornography. As normal human beings, when we are intimate with our mate it is because we are showing our love and affection for that person and making love to them is one way to strengthen our bond that we have with them. On the other hand, a Narc can sleep with you and not even have a connection.

13
NARCISSISTS ARE RUDE PEOPLE

Have you ever found yourself apologizing for something the narcissist said or did to someone? They walk this earth as if they are untouchable. They can say the cruelest things to people. They do not care who you are. The crazy thing about them being cruel to other people is that when you say things back to them defending yourself you fracture their ego. If you fracture their ego, they will never forgive nor forget what you said to them. They will hold that grudge while plotting to take you down. They are the most vindictive people you will ever run into on earth. Another part of their behavior that bothers me is when they say mean things to us and then we confront them, and they try to make it seem like they were just joking or tell us that we are being too sensitive. They mean exactly what they say. I remember one time he told me that I had taught him so much during our relationship that he was probably dangerous to me. I looked at him in his eyes and said, A student is never smarter than their teacher. If you could have been a fly on the wall to see the expression on his face after that comment I made it was priceless. I know I fractured his ego. If they can get away with their behaviors, they will continue to be disrespectful because that is who they truly are.

14

THE CONFUSION YOU GET WHEN DEALING WITH A NARCISSIST

Ladies, I know you understand what I am about to say. These men are hot and cold. One minute they will show you the world taking you places you have never been before and doing things for you that no other man has ever done for you. They make you promises that you honestly believe because they can sound so convincing when they say them. I have witnessed my ex-narc looking me in my face without a smile lying to me and I knew he was lying but somehow, I started gaslighting myself because I was so in love with that man and was not ready to let him go. They get in your head saying things like, I never loved anyone the way I love you. It is something about you that makes you different from the past woman I have dated... Knowing they are lying to you. I have learned not to listen to them when they say I love you because it is all part of their game. Instead, you must pay attention to their actions. You can say you love someone but if your actions are disrespectful on so many levels you do not love them. On the other hand, they can be so cold and treat you like an enemy. They will stay out all night with other women not caring if you are at home with the kids or worried about them. Whenever you want to talk to them about something that is bothering you, or want to have an intellectual conversation, they can be extremely childish with their response, leaving you confused about where the relationship is going. When they realize that you are starting to pull away from them that is when breadcrumbing will come into play. They will try to pull you back in by making plans to take you on a nice vacation, dinner, movie, or to a spot that you mentioned to them a while back at the beginning of the relationship. It is funny ladies, how they try to gaslight us about the things they have done to us in the past that hurt us. They will say they don't remember are that it didn't happen, but they can remember all the things you said to them at the beginning of the relationship. Trust me ladies they do not forget things they just choose not take accountability for what they have done to you.

15

TRYING TO KEEP YOU AWAY FROM YOUR FAMILY AND FRIENDS

When they ask us questions about our family and friends, we tell them about all our family secrets and things we have gone through with our friends because you view them as your significant other and feel like you should be able to talk to them about anything. In your head you are like this is my best friend/ spouse or mate. In their heads they are thinking this is something that I will use on her later to sabotage her relationship with her family and friends. One of the reasons they try to keep you away from family and friends is because they are mistreating and abusing you. They know that your family and friends will say something to them or try to convince you to leave them. Your family and friends will tell you that you deserve better. They are no fools, trust me we were not their first rodeo. As a reminder, please be mindful of what you say to them if you choose to stay in the relationship. I am not here to tell you to leave your partner because I understand sometimes it is not that easy due to your circumstances. I stayed for over a decade before I did my research on Narcissistic Abuse. I never knew people like them existed. I am just here to give you information on what life is like dealing with a narcissistic person. Again, my ex-narc called my family members telling them all the bedroom conversations we had about them after I left him and tried to go to my family and friends for support. He also tried to turn them against me by trying to pretend that I was the crazy one oh yes, they will make people think that you are crazy while painting the picture that they are the victim, and you are the abuser.

16

PLAYING THE VICTIM ROLE

Honey, let me tell you these men have masks... *chuckle*.

They will destroy everything in their path: spouse, children, mate, friends, their family members, the list can go on and on. However, they will still pretend to act like the victim. They are so good at pretending to be the victim they will have you questioning if you are the narcissist. Ladies, you are not a narcissist. There is such a thing as reactive abuse. You are only trying to protect yourself from their abuse towards you. They always try to justify their actions. I remember the first time I left him. It was due to his constantly cheating with other women and staying out all times of night coming back and forth to the home we shared with our children and the children having to watch this kind of behavior. Also, with him lacking in his responsibilities as a father and husband. Ladies, how many of you know when you leave them, they will call, beg, cry, and make promises to be a better man and because of the kind of heart we have we believe they will change and end up going back to them hoping and praying that it will go back to how they made us feel in the beginning. That will never happen. Each time you go back the relationship will get worse and worse. It is a matter of fact that they stop respecting you and at that point whatever they are doing they no longer try to hide it. So let me tell you about one of the episodes I had with him. As I was saying earlier, I left and he begged me to come back, which I did after being gone for four months. I remember him handing me his phone to read an important message from a doctor's appointment he had and while I had his phone a message came through from another woman telling him that she just wanted to let him know that she was in love with him. I tried to hold my anger in and asked him if we could step outside so we could have a discussion instead of talking in front of our children. I told him that he had just received a message that had just come through his phone. I handed the phone back to him and he viewed it and said what the**** as if he was shocked. He instantly got mad at me for what he was doing. At that point I got upset and left home by myself to think about what my actions should be. When I came back, he left and stayed gone for hours before returning. My guess was that he went to her house. The next day I got up, got my children dressed and packed our belongings. We shared a car together, so he did not have any idea that I was going to drive it 12 hours away to get back home to my family. I called my brother and asked him if he could send me $100, for gas to get back home and the reason I was leaving my husband. My brother sent me the money. I had $1 on my debit card so I knew I could fill the car up using $1 and pressing credit at the gas pump so I did. I remember meeting up with him before we left to give him something important that I knew he needed before leaving. My children were in the car and knew what was going on so as he walked over to the car our daughter was crying in the back seat because she knew we were leaving him he just didn't know so he was trying to understand why she was so upset but his phone started ringing and because he was so close to the car it connected the call to the Bluetooth in the car and the name of the female that sent the message the following night showed up on the screen in the car my child said mom look I saw her name and told him that I was going to answer the call. This man ran so fast away from the car that the car speakers could not connect. Then he looked over at me with this irritating grin. Ladies, if you know the grin you can imagine it on his face. They all have that fake evil smile. I left there and hit the highway. I want to say that around 4 hours into our drive, he started calling our phones asking where we were. I would tell him we were Door Dashing and he would say okay, what time are you coming back? After not hearing from us for hours he knew that was not true because I had left him a few times before and he knew if I was gone for hours at a time, I would not come back for months. He started to lose his cool. He started threatening me saying he was going to call the police to have me arrested for kidnapping the children and stealing the car. I was terrified but I told my children I was not going back to that hell hole. It did not matter what happened to me if I got them to my family safe. After a while of him calling me and making threats he realized we were gone and we were not coming back. He tried love bombing me again with his apologies saying how sorry he was and that he loved us and wanted his family back. We stayed with my family for three months. He called every day begging eventually I blocked him. He started calling our children's phones trying to find information about me. It was like this man was losing his mind. I would talk to him over the phone and I could hear him hyperventilating. Even though this man was not a great father nor husband he was always a provider. I will give him that. That is why he knew I would have to come back to him because I did not have that family support. Eventually we came back to him and he promised me that he had learned his lesson and that he was a changed man and realized his mistakes and promised me that he wasn't going to hurt me or the children again. That he just wanted his family back. When we came back to him, even though we did not have a stable place to stay we lived in decent hotels for months.

The kids thought they were living their best life because most of the places had a jacuzzi and an indoor swimming pool. I'm so grateful as a mother that my children found joy in our time of crisis. I did not complain because I loved him, and I felt like the family was together and we had a roof over our heads. Shortly after us coming back the same behaviors started to resurface. One day he left his bank statement on the hotel dresser and left for hours. I grabbed the papers and started to read them. I saw Cash App transactions to and from women including the one that I had left him for. We moved out of the hotel into an apartment together. He started staying out all night again. I spoke to him about it and he did not seem to care. That is when I made up my mind. I cannot do this anymore with him. I filed for a divorce and started to set clear and firm boundaries and that is when the mask completely came off. This man showed me a side of him that I had never seen in the entire years that I was with him. He became so disrespectful with his words and actions. He said to me I tell women what they want to hear to get what I want. I have been with this man while he admires other women head to toe in front of me. He has told me he has broken the strongest women down and so much more. He had the nerves to tell me it was my fault and the reason he was messing with another woman. He said because I left him, and he was lonely she took a liking to him and helped him out while I was gone. I told him you act like I just woke up and left you; you know why I left you because of the way you were treating me. I told him you are making people think that you are the victim when in all I am the victim.

17

HEALTH ISSUES DUE TO NARCISSIST ABUSE

Dealing with a narcissist will affect your mental and physical health. I cannot count the times I thought I was going to lose my mind. I remember walking through the house praying to God asking God to protect my mind because I felt like I was losing it every day. I could not sleep or eat properly. My stress level and anxiety were through the roof. I stayed going back and forth to the doctor complaining to them that something was going on with my body, but I could not put my finger on it. I heard that he was going around town telling everybody that I was going crazy and the reason I continued going to the hospital. Never once told them what he was doing to me behind closed doors that caused my anxiety to be through the roof. My blood pressure stayed high, and my psoriasis flared like crazy throughout my body. Ladies, if you are not familiar with psoriasis it is a skin condition that appears on the body looking like white scales and patches but one of the triggers is stress. When I was going through my crisis, he never went to the hospital with me. He dropped me off at the emergency room door then told me to call him when I was ready for him to pick me up. I did not think anything of it while my heart and mind were in the relationship but as soon as I started to pull away, I realized that when you love someone you stand by their side in whatever storm they are going through. I have always been to every doctor's appointment or hospital visit he ever had if he allowed me to go. In fact, on one visit I stepped in to inform the doctor about his medical complications. I will never forget the doctor telling him that he was lucky to have a wife that cared about his health. One day while we were riding in the car, a conversation came up about what the doctor said to him. He made the comment to me saying there are other women out here that care about their mates' health. I took that as if he had met someone else and felt that she cared more about him than I did. Ladies, I am here to tell you that once I pulled away from him my mental and physical health improved. I still must deal with him because we share kids together, but I keep the conversations about the children and set strong boundaries when I see him.

18

THEY USE RELIGION TO MANIPULATE YOU

I grew up as a Christian. I did not have any inclinations about other beliefs. When I met my boyfriend at the time religion and our beliefs were not a topic but we both agreed on believing in a higher power. After I gave birth to our first child, that is when he told me that he was a Muslim. Still, I did not have a problem with his beliefs because it did not affect mine. A few years down the line, when he told me that children must take on their father's beliefs, that is when I started to investigate Islam because I wanted to see what he was going to be teaching our children. After doing my research Islamic teaching speaks about peace. The problem came when he tried to use his beliefs to manipulate me into submission after he started to abuse me mentally and emotionally. I loved this man so much I was willing to convert to Islam but because of his actions I rejected the teachings. I want to add that it does not matter what belief or religion a person has if the heart is not pure. One of the reasons I stayed with him for so long was because I believed God honored marriages.

19
THE PAIN YOU FEEL IN YOUR HEART FROM LOVING THE NARCISSIST

Ladies, I do not know where to start when it comes to the pain we feel from loving them. My heart became numb over a period. I do not understand how a person could inflict so much pain on an individual and not have a care in this world. I get it, toxic people hurt others but the cruelty they bring to the table is like a prison sentence. They throw the I love you word around like it is trash. That word used to get to me all the time because when normal people say I love you to a person we mean it with all our beings. That means. I am your rider through thick and thin and whatever we go through in life it is all good if we have each other. Oh, baby let me tell you, when they say I love you it is because there is something that they want or have done to us. These guys do not love anyone. I used to say they only loved themselves, but I take that back because if they loved themselves, they would not participate in destructive behaviors. I have tossed and turned in my sleep so many times I cannot count. I got out of bed at night looking out of the window trying to see if he made it home or if he was going to pull up only to be disappointed because he stayed out all night. I remember when he got there, he would have this smirk on his face nonchalantly. One thing that I have learned is that when they find someone new or think they have found true love nothing and no one will keep them home. You can beg them to spend time with you. They will still leave you and the kids at home to get to the other woman. That is when I realized that he was not capable of loving me the way I deserve. I knew then that I was dealing with someone that was different from any other man that I had ever dealt with before. The problem was I could not leave this man even though he caused me so much pain. I would bury the pain to the back of my mind and still love and want this man. Ladies, if this could help one person, I would have done my job. We are wasting our time because you cannot love them enough and feel sorry for them because each time you let your guard down on them, they are going to hit you every time. The sweet nothing they say to us to keep us coming back to them they do not mean it. You can have an enjoyable day with them today then tomorrow morning you wake up to a different person. We must start putting ourselves first in our lives. It is not our job to fix other people's brokenness.

We must learn self-love and settle for nothing less. If they say I am going to get help because I love you and do not want to lose you. This is one phase they use to manipulate you into staying with them after you decide that you have had enough of their behaviors. If they want help, we do not have to stick around while they get themselves together. We can work on ourselves and realize that we deserve so much better. Another thing that I realized is that once I really built the courage to walk away all the things that I had pushed to the back of my mind came forward and reminded me of every painful moment I endured while being with him and how I never wanted to feel that pain ever again in my life. Even though sometimes I still think of him I know that is because of the trauma and bond we had together. I quickly remind myself how painful and lonely it is being with a narcissist and that thought is short lived.

20

BE WILLING TO RISK IT ALL
TO GET AWAY.

When I made up my mind that I was willing to walk away from my marriage with only my children, and if we had to live in a shelter, I was not going back to him, that's when things started to turn around for me. I was able to give him the cold shoulder. He tried everything to upset me and even though he did some hurtful things to me like introducing our child to one of his supplies and her coming back to tell me that he asked her to get out of the car and hug this lady that she had never met before. He also told her not to tell me because I was going to act crazy. I'll never forget the day he came to my place to see the children. When he was getting ready to leave I called him outside to tell him that I knew our daughter had met his supply but I was not mad and that I told our daughter to be nice to the young lady and as long as she doesn't do anything to harm her I'm fine with her, because I know me and her father are no longer together so we must move on with our lives. I smiled and waved to him as he nervously walked off while asking me if I needed anything. I replied no thank you. He did not know how to manage what I had said to him. He continued to call, send text messages, show up at the house unannounced, and try to get information about me from our children. It then hit me that life is a game to them and the best way to bet them at their game is not to play it. I changed my number. He only had access to me through our children's phones or via emails and if he sent emails that I viewed as nonsense I would not respond.

21

THE PAIN YOU FEEL AFTER GOING TO NO CONTACT

I want you to understand that once you have remained no contact and have moved on with your life you will go through a range of emotions. There were days I wanted to pick up the phone and call him to tell him to come back home or cuss him out for the pain and wasted time I spent in the relationship but kept the strength to overcome the urge. I continued to wonder if there was anything that I could have done differently to save the relationship. I started blaming myself for staying in the relationship for so long. Eventually, reality started to set in and then the blindfold came off. That is when my mind started to recall everything the narcissist had done to me that I had buried in the back of my mind. I realized this man had treated me so cruelly and said the meanest things to me. Till this day I am still in disbelief that a person can treat a human being this cruelly and have no remorse for their actions.

The strength you carry from being a survivor of narcissistic abuse.

Being in and getting out of a relationship with a narcissist is one of the hardest battles anyone can face in life. We have been through a strong storm without an umbrella. The pain was unthinkable. We have felt alone, abandoned, misunderstood, angry, scared, confused, and betrayed. The truth of the matter is going through these painful experiences has taught us things about ourselves we never knew. We have learned our worth and how to self-love. I have tapped into my purpose in life. We have rediscovered our passion and dreams in life. We have learned how to protect ourselves from not ignoring red flags. I cannot speak for everyone else, but I have learned how to give my problems and burdens to God because I promise you, I do not think I would have made it out if I did not surrender it all to God.

22

FINAL REMARKS AND THE POWER OF FORGIVENESS

I never thought I would be authoring this book about narcissist abuse. Never imagined that this would be one of my testimonies in life.

Ladies, because I am on my healing journey, and the only thing I want to do at this point in my life is to do what I think is pleasing to God, so I have forgiven my ex-narc, mother, ex-friends, and family members. I realize that forgiving them is for me. I cannot move forward in life without letting go of anger and pain. I hope this helps someone.

I listen to Sarah Jakes she is the daughter of T.D. Jakes, all the time on You- Tube and one day what she said I knew that was God's way of helping me heal from my pain. She said when we leave our position someone else must take that position... What I got from that was when we met the narcissist, a part of us was broken and abused from our childhood trauma which were the reason we tolerated their abuse for so long but because we are an awakening empath now, we realize that we deserve better and have figured out our worth. We are no longer giving them anymore supplies. They must move on to someone else so that person can face and heal from their childhood trauma and break the cycle just like we had to do.

I am also glad God led me to Dr. Ramani's YouTube channel. Listening to her gave me the strength that I needed to change my situation for the better. It is scary to step out on faith and walk away from someone that you genuinely loved and created a traumatizing bond with. I remember saying I do not know why I stayed in this relationship for so long. God I know there is a lesson in this. Then I heard someone say and I never forgot (We were with them to show them how to love and they taught us how to self-love) however do not confuse this statement with thinking that the more love you give them that they will eventually love you back. That is not the case with them. They are so broken and must heal as well.

I am glad I have a great support group on Facebook called "Trauma Bond and Recovery". I also want to give a shot out to **Mami So True, Hario Ovadtop, Mental Healness.** You guys have done an amazing job during my healing process. I have spent hours getting free therapy from you all. I still get weak, but I go to my support group or listen to my free therapy and within minutes I get the strength to keep fighting. I also started my very own group on Facebook called Healing one day at a time from Narcissist abuse and have decided to become a **One on One life Coach for Narcissist Abuse.**

To book Zoom sessions you contact me through email Patricia1on1lifecoach@gmail.com

My mission in life is to get this information out here until there are no more suffering people from narcissist abuse.

Patricia Clark

9 7 9 8 8 9 3 8 3 6 0 7 3